Print, Paint & Ink

OVER 20 MODERN CRAFT PROJECTS FOR YOU AND YOUR HOME

Print, Paint & Ink

OVER 20 MODERN CRAFT PROJECTS FOR YOU AND YOUR HOME

ANDIE POWERS & EMILY GROSSE
OF *Assemble* SHOP & STUDIO

The Taunton Press

To Christian and Alice, who taught me what I really want out of life.
To my parents, who have always encouraged creativity and joy each and every day.
—*Andie Powers*

To Will, Henry, and George, who have created our home and filled it with joy.
To my parents, who taught me how success and happiness are made and found.
—*Emily Grosse*

The Taunton Press
Inspiration for hands-on living®

The Taunton Press, Inc.
63 South Main Street, PO Box 5506
Newtown, CT 06470-5506
e-mail: tp@taunton.com

Editors: Renee Neiger, Tim Stobierski
Copy Editor: Diane Sinitsky
Art Director: Rosalind Loeb Wanke
Cover and Interior design: Rita Sowins
Layout: Sandra Mahlstedt
Illustrator: Michelle Beilner
Photographer: Jaquilyn Shumate

The following names/manufacturers appearing in *Print, Paint & Ink* are trademarks:
Americana®; Ceramcoat®; ColorBox®; Crate & Barrel®; DMC®; Fabriano®; Goop®;
Hero Arts®; Jacquard®; Micron®; Paper Source®; Scotch®; Sharpie®; Speedball®;
Spirograph®; X-Acto®

Library of Congress Cataloging-in-Publication Data

Names: Powers, Andie, author. | Grosse, Emily, author.
Title: Print, paint & ink : over 20 modern craft projects for you and your
  home / Andie Powers & Emily Grosse.
Other titles: Print, paint and ink
Description: Newtown, CT : Taunton Press, Inc., [2016]
Identifiers: LCCN 2016012063 | ISBN 9781631863134
Subjects: LCSH: Handicraft. | House furnishings.
Classification: LCC TT157 .P728 2016 | DDC 745.5--dc23
LC record available at https://lccn.loc.gov/2016012063

Printed in the United States of America
10 9 8 7 6 5 4 3 2 1

ACKNOWLEDGMENTS

So much gratitude and love to our amazing creative team, photographer Jaquilyn Shumate and illustrator Michelle Beilner, for their hard work, time, and support in making this book a reality.

Special thanks to Sam Spencer and Dominic Williamson, Isabelle and Nick Robertson, Rachel and Jimmy Nichols, Matthew Sumi, and the Boswell family for allowing us to photograph our projects in their beautiful homes. And thanks to our agent, Alison Fargis, for wisdom and working hard on our behalf, Lidia Flanigan for styling assistance, and Travis Shumate for editing photos late into the night.

CONTENTS

INTRODUCTION

When we met in 2006, we would have never guessed that the next 10 years would become such a creative adventure. We found ourselves in Seattle by way of two very different paths. Used to the nomadic lifestyle that children with parents in the Armed Forces are usually accustomed to, Andie traveled to Seattle by way of a string of cities including Boston and Los Angeles, gathering a taste for modern art and a keen eye for design. Emily moved to Seattle from Chicago with a wealth of knowledge and education in traditional crafting techniques and a Midwestern affinity for making a house into a home. In the early days of our friendship, as fellow employees of a chain craft and stationery store, we spent most of our time lending a hand to wayward customers and teaching workshops in a corporate setting. We soon realized we shared a pipe dream to open a shop of our own. We envisioned a brick-and-mortar shop, workshop space, and gallery where we could teach our crafting skills and curate gorgeous works of art and products by independent artisans. With our stars aligned, in 2009 we opened Assemble Gallery & Studio in the Phinneywood area of Seattle. It was a dream come true for two girls who couldn't believe their luck. We met hundreds of amazing friends, designers, and artists, all who have made our second dream a bit easier to reach: writing this book.

From our work at Assemble, we gained experience working with crafters of all levels on projects that were lively and fresh, using many types of traditional crafting techniques with a contemporary twist. Due to the popularity of our Assemble Stamp Sets and print-making workshops, we decided to devote the entirety of this book to stamping, inking, dyeing, and otherwise getting your fingers messy with color. This book was born out of the desire to create colorful, fun, and relatable projects that can be showcased in a modern home or lifestyle. It's one thing to create something beautiful—it's another to find a place for it in your life and home.

In terms of where *we* call home, we find Seattle and the Pacific Northwest to be a huge source of inspiration in craft and design. This area is such an intricate and rich treasure trove of natural colors and textures—boasting elements of mountains, forest, sea, and city all so close together. Seattle also has a deeply rooted Scandinavian history, so we include some of their elements of minimalism mixed with traditional craft. The Pacific Northwest has been rewritten as both of our forever homes, and our sense of newfound place has colored many of the projects in this book, as well as nostalgia for the homes that we have left. We hope you are inspired to create these pieces and enjoy finding special places for them in your life, too!

~ Andie & Emily

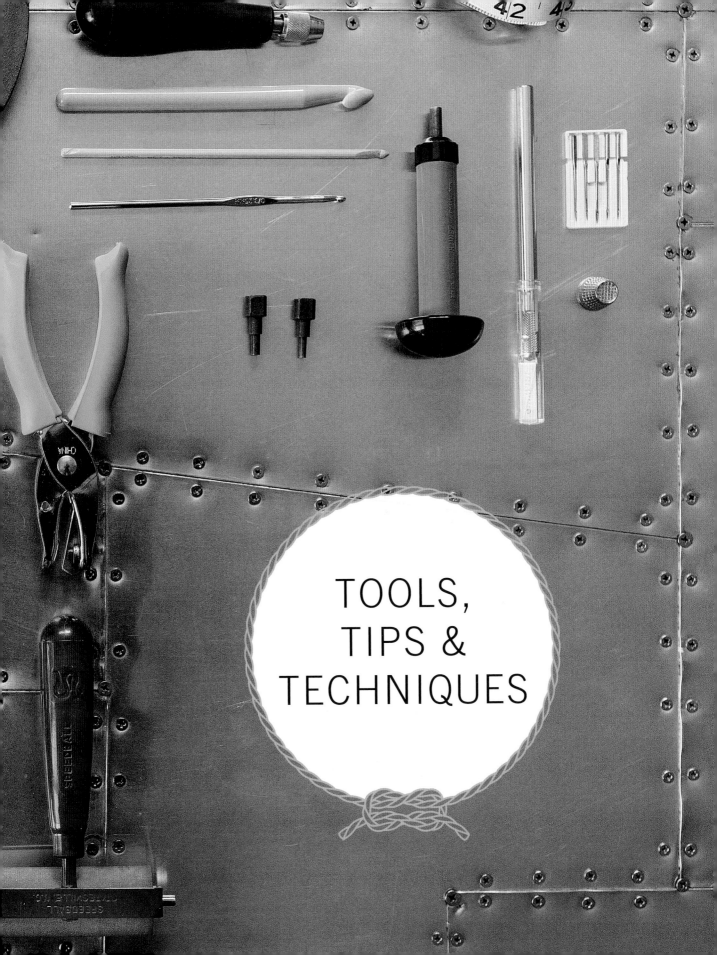

TOOLS,
TIPS &
TECHNIQUES

TOOLS

There are many questions that come up when you start a new project, mainly because there are so many options out there! Do you always need a brayer when you stamp? Should you use textile ink or a pigment pad? And what in the world is a Japanese screw punch? We will tell you how to use what you need, suggest simple alternatives, and give you as many tips as we can to make your work successful and fun.

We have spent years teaching fellow crafters everything we know and in return have learned valuable tidbits from our students. These notes about the tools we use will help any crafter decide what to use and how. We love using quality tools, so here you will find an alphabetical listing of the tools we find most valuable.

TOOL TERMS AND DEFINITIONS

Adhesives Polyvinyl acetate (PVA) is a common craft glue, especially for bookbinding. It dries quickly, is clear and flexible, and is pH-neutral and archival, which makes it a perfect option for paper projects. Although PVA is our favorite choice of adhesive for many projects, we also suggest using double-sided tape, wood glue, rubber cement, and hot glue for a few others.

Bone folder A bone folder is a hand tool used to score, fold, crease, and smooth paper. Bone folders average about 6 in. long and have one dull point and one rounded edge. They are most commonly used in bookbinding or origami. Although traditionally carved from animal bone, there are synthetic versions available, too.

Brayer Brayers are traditionally used for printmaking in two ways: to roll ink evenly onto large surfaces or to apply even pressure on the backside of a stamp or block. Using a brayer in either way helps ensure a more uniform print. Brayers can also be used to smooth out air bubbles between layers of paper and glue.

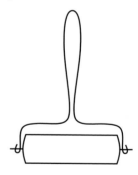

Embroidery floss Used for embroidery, cross-stitch, and other needlework, embroidery floss comes in a variety of colors and materials. Floss usually consists of six strands of thread intertwined together, which can be separated for a more delicate thread.

Embroidery hoop This is a frame made up of an inner hoop and an outer hoop, which is used to hold material in place while embroidering. You can find hoops in lightweight wood or plastic, usually ranging from 3 in. to 12 in. in diameter. When using one, your entire image does not need to fit completely inside the hoop area, but the material must be larger than the hoop itself.

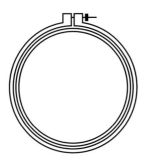

Embroidery needles Also known as crewel needles, embroidery needles are medium-size stitching needles with a long eye and a sharp point. They come in a variety of sizes, which are commonly differentiated by numbers 1 through 12. The higher the number is, the smaller the needle.

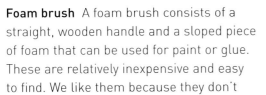

Foam brush A foam brush consists of a straight, wooden handle and a sloped piece of foam that can be used for paint or glue. These are relatively inexpensive and easy to find. We like them because they don't leave bristle marks behind and can be easily cleaned with soap and water. Foam brushes come in a variety of sizes from 1 in. to 4 in.

Hole punch A manual hole punch is used for making many sizes and shapes of holes in paper. Hole punch sizes range from very small to large and have a variety of reaches, meaning the amount of space from the edge of the page that you can punch into the paper. The capacity varies from a single sheet to several. For the projects in this book, we used a standard ¼-in. circle and a ⅛-in. triangle.

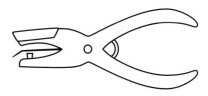

Ink pad This is an ink-soaked pad, usually set in a plastic tray, for inking up a craft stamp. Dye-based and pigment-based ink pads are the two types that are most readily available. Dye pad inks dry quickly and work on nonporous surfaces. Pigment pad inks work well on paper and fabric but take longer to dry.

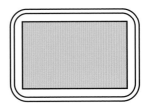

Iron An iron is one of the most important tools in a crafter's toolkit. Use it to smooth or steam out wrinkles in your fabrics to ensure a much better finished project. We use an iron to heat-set ink on fabric. Remember to use a scrap fabric barrier between your work and the iron, especially when heat-setting ink, to avoid transferring marks to other pieces you iron.

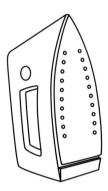

Japanese screw punch A screw punch, also known as a Japanese book drill, is a hand-held tool that bores holes through paper, cardboard, foam, fabric, wood, and leather. Sometimes made of wood and brass, or plastic and steel, most punches come with interchangeable tips with different-size holes. Some screw punches require you to grip the handle in your palm and twist. For other versions, you just push straight down.

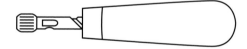

Linoleum block Traditional block printer's linoleum is made of linseed oil, cork, and resin to create a thin, pliable surface to carve into. There are soft and hard versions of linoleum, ranging in thickness. The softer ones are easier to carve but hold less detail and deteriorate more quickly. The harder

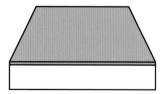

variety can require more force to carve, but you can get greater detail with smaller cuts. Some blocks are mounted on wood, others have a woven backing, and some come in sheets.

Linoleum cutter A linoleum cutter consists of a handle and blade that is used to carve through linoleum blocks, rubber-stamping blocks, and other synthetic printmaker's blocks. There are wooden handles and plastic handles with clutches to slide in removable blades. Blades vary in size and shape, from small V-notches to large U-shapes. Speedball® is a recognizable brand with lots of interchangeable options. You can use palm-grip wood gouges and chisels as well.

Paper awl A paper awl, also called a paper piercer, is a handle with a long, pointed tip to stab through sheets of paper. Awls come with either plastic or wooden handles, and the metal piercer can vary in thickness. Paper awls found at the craft store will be thinner and sharper than an awl you would find at a home improvement store, but those work for most projects, too.

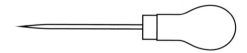

Porcelain pens Belonging to the paint pen family, porcelain pens contain specially formulated ink to last on glass, ceramic, porcelain, and metal. They are usually spring-loaded with fiber tips. Porcelain pens come in fine, medium, and blunt tips in a handful of standard colors that are transparent, semitransparent, or opaque. Most varieties include the option to oven-bake the piece to set the ink.

Precision knife Also called a pen knife or an X-Acto® knife, a precision knife is used to create intricate and detailed cuts in paper, cardstock, linoleum, leather, and other materials. If you are a beginner, choose a precision knife with a rubber grip to avoid slippage. Blades usually come covered in a thin oil to prevent rusting. Carefully wipe the blade with a towel before installing it in your knife.

Rulers Rulers are a must for your toolkit. **Acrylic** rulers are most helpful when measuring and cutting fabric because you can see through them, which allows you to double-check that the pattern is in the right place and know exactly where the rotary tool will land. A **metal** ruler is preferred when measuring and cutting paper so that you don't risk slicing through an acrylic or wood ruler with your tool.

Sandpaper Different "grits" of sandpaper are useful for different projects. The lower the number of the sandpaper, the rougher the grit is. For stripping and deep sanding, 40 to 60 grit would be best. For the delicate wood projects in this book, stick with superfine sandpaper, which is around 360 to 600 grit.

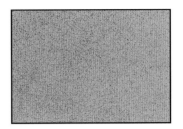

Scissors We keep several types of scissors in our toolkit. We use large, sharp metal shears for cutting fabric and detail scissors for paper cuts. It is important to keep fabric scissors for use on fabric only and paper scissors for paper. Otherwise, your shears will dull very quickly.

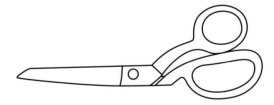

Self-healing cutting mat Another staple for the crafter's workstation is the self-healing cutting mat. This vinyl mat, usually equipped with a 1-in. graph for cutting straight lines, absorbs cuts by a precision knife or rotary cutter and minimizes the effect of the cut, leaving your workspace line-free. Some mats come with curved and straight-angle cutting guides and can be found in a variety of sizes and colors.

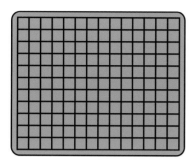

Sewing machine A sewing machine helps fabric-based projects move along quickly, by connecting fabric with thread at the push of a button. All brands carry a wide range of models with differing features at varying price points. Some of the projects in this book require minimal sewing machine knowledge (such as making a straight stitch).

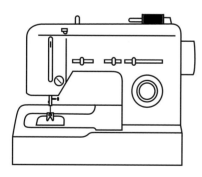

Sewing needles Hand-sewing needles are tools with a sharp point at one end to pierce through fabric and an eye at the blunt end to hold thread. Sharps are the most common type of hand-sewing needle and are available in many thicknesses. Embroidery needles are nearly identical to sharps but have a longer eye to accommodate multiple threads or floss.

Stencil brush A stencil brush, or stipple brush, is used to apply ink onto a surface over a cut stencil. Stencil brushes are often round with a flat bottom. They can be made of foam or of natural or synthetic bristles. The flat bottom helps to apply ink without getting any under the surface of the stencil.

Textile ink Textile paint, or textile color, is usually a water-based ink used for printing on fabric. Brand to brand and color to color, the texture and viscosity will vary. Be sure to look for paints that can be washed. Textile ink is not the same as block-printing or screen-printing ink. Choosing the exact brand and type depends on your project materials and desired outcome. Our favorite all-purpose textile paint is Jacquard® brand.

TIPS AND ADVICE FOR PROJECTS USING PAPER AND GLUE

A lot of us have been crafting with paper and glue since preschool. Since then, we've upgraded our materials and perfected techniques that we hope will help you, too.

PAPER CHOICES

Text weight Typically used for interior pages, text weight ranges between 20 lb. (computer printer paper) and 60 lb. (letterhead).

Cover weight This thicker paper is typically used for exterior pages or covers, around 80 lb., or the thickness of an index card or manila folder.

Cardstock Even thicker still, cardstock is considered anything over 90 lb. It's perfect for business cards and invitations.

Recycled Paper bags and magazines make great eco-friendly choices for a lot of our projects. We encourage using and reusing whatever you might have on hand. Recycled papers may not be archival, however, and may warp and discolor more quickly.

BOOKBINDING TERMS AND DEFINITIONS

Grain The direction in which most of the fibers in a piece of paper are aligned is the grain. In bookbinding, it should run parallel to the spine. Folding with the grain will result in a smooth and crisp line. If you fold against the grain, your paper may crack along the fold or make an uneven edge. You can find the grain direction by gently bending the paper horizontally and then vertically. The direction with less resistance is parallel to the grain.

Jig A jig is a guide for making evenly spaced holes through paper. A traditional binding jig is made of wood and clamps many pages together at once while you bore holes. For the projects in this book, you can print our jig templates on cardstock, which you can hold or tape in place.

Scoring Scoring is the act of creating a line in the paper that will help the paper fold. Usually, you score by running a bone folder along a ruler to make a depression in the paper. It is ideal to score parallel to the paper's grain.

Signature Two or more sheets of paper stacked and folded as a group to create a section of a book is called a signature. For handmade books, there can be any number of sheets to a signature.

Station When bookbinding, these are the points at which sewing reverses direction from "in" to "out" through a text block. Some just call them holes!

BOOKBINDING TIPS

Bookbinding is traditionally a precise and technical craft. The projects in this book incorporate more room for error and allow creative choices in materials.

∗ A guillotine-style paper cutter is helpful when cutting pages to precise measurement. For our binding projects, a ruler and precision knife will work just fine, but if you enjoy the process (and we hope you do!), consider investing in a 12-in. x 12-in. paper cutter to save time and get nearly perfectly uniform results.

• Remember to keep the grain direction of all materials parallel to the book spine. This will create a more stable book and help guard against uneven warping.

• The spine of a book can be glued and/or sewn together depending on the style. To poke holes through your paper, it is common to use an awl, also called a paper piercer. An awl will displace the surrounding paper to create a hole and is most often used in signature binding. A screw punch, also called a stab punch, will bore through and remove paper to create a hole and is most often used in Japanese-style binding. Both awls and punches have a variety of thicknesses to choose from.

MORE ABOUT ADHESIVES

We use all sorts of adhesives: PVA, glue sticks, double-sided tape, washi tape, rubber cement, and hot glue. We suggest the best option for each project in the directions.

A little glue goes a long way, especially with PVA. Usually, you need just enough to adhere two bits together. The bond will strengthen while drying and curing. Drying time can vary from moments to hours. A single layer of PVA dries within several minutes but can take 24 hours or more to fully cure. Keep drying or curing paper projects weighted under heavy books to ward off warping.

CARING FOR PAPER PROJECTS

Paper responds negatively to humidity, acidity, and time by warping and discoloring. You can use recycled and found materials for most of our projects. But if you are hoping for an archival finished product, make sure your paper and glue choices are pH-neutral. The packaging should say if it is archival or pH-neutral. Store paper pieces flat and weighted when not being used, if possible.

TECHNIQUES AND ADVICE FOR PROJECTS USING FABRIC

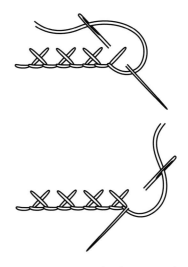

We could spend hours at our favorite fabric stores, where there is endless inspiration. We've collected some key tips to help your sewing and fabric-based printing projects go from shopping cart to art!

FABRIC AND FIBER MATERIALS

Cotton fabric We recommend using 100% cotton for general sewing projects. Cotton is easy to work with and care for, and it is most gentle on the environment. Remember to wash, dry, and iron all of your fabric before measuring and cutting your pieces. You want to be sure your finished projects won't shrink or warp later on.

HAND-SEWING AND EMBROIDERY STITCHES

Here are a few simple hand-sewing techniques for the projects that use fabric. You can definitely hem using a sewing machine, but hand stitches and embroidery are not difficult to try out, and the results add a softness and handmade touch.

Cross blanket stitch This is a variation on the traditional blanket stitch used as a simple hem when sewing or as a decorative edging on embroidery. When stitching, you'll be working between two parallel lines from left to right.

1. Thread your needle and start at the bottom left. Insert the needle to the right on

top and bring it out the bottom, slanting to the left. Make sure the working thread is under the point, and pull through to complete the stitch.

2. Insert the needle on the top to the left of the previous cross. Bring it out the bottom below the top of the first stitch with the working thread under the point.

3. Pull the needle through gently to complete the cross.

Long and short stitch This is a variation on the traditional blanket stitch, simply by changing the length of the stitches in a repeating pattern. You can use this stitch on hems or as a decorative edging. You'll work from left to right, keeping the spacing between stitches consistent.

1. Begin by bringing the needle to the front on the bottom line and insert it at the top, slightly to the right, keeping the thread under the tip of the needle.

2. Pull the thread through the fabric, over the top of the working thread. Gently pull the thread to form a loop at the bottom.

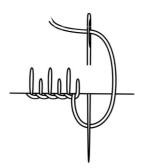

3. Continue toward the right, rotating the pattern of one short upright stitch and then one long stitch.

4. Tie off at the back of the work when you are finished.

Satin stitch This stitch is used in embroidery as a filler stitch. The flat lines of thread or floss can cover larger areas of fabric than other stitches. You can also choose to angle each stitch slightly.

1. Pull the needle up and out until the knot reaches the back of the fabric.

2. Push the needle from the front to the back, at the opposite point on the border, straight across from where you started.

3. You'll start your next stitch right next to the first, going from the back to the front. All of your stitches will start on the same side of the border and end on the opposite side.

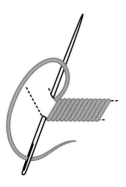

STITCHING TOOL TIPS

There are endless varieties of embroidery needles, designed to suit small or large needlework on all sorts of surfaces. We have found that most all-purpose needles will do for our stitching projects. You want a needle that is thin enough to go through your fabric without leaving large holes, yet still has an eye big enough for several threads of floss.

CARING FOR FABRIC AND FIBER PIECES

Fabric-based projects that have been printed or dyed need a little extra care. Once textile ink has been heat-set, most cotton can be washed and dried with your regular linens. Fabric that is hand-dyed should be washed separately and in cold water. If a piece has been embroidered, wash it by hand and lay flat to dry. All fabrics should be prewashed before dying, printing, or sewing so you don't need to worry about shrinking or colors running.

HOW TO SEW A ¼-IN. SEAM

To make a ¼-in. seam while attaching two pieces of fabric, line up the two straight edges that will be sewn together. The pattern will tell you if they should be right or wrong sides together. Measure in ¼ in. from the edge along the entire length to be sewn—this will be the line of stitches. You can mark the fabric with a fabric marker or place pins along the ¼-in. line as a guide. Sew by hand or machine along the ¼-in. line to create the seam.

TIPS AND ADVICE FOR PROJECTS USING STAMPS AND INK

We use a variety of simple techniques and materials to get you started on your stamp and ink projects. With just a few basic materials, you will have access to endless possibilities for designing your own prints and patterns. These techniques will get you started in the right direction.

TRANSFERRING TEMPLATES

You'll be photocopying lots of images, stencils, and templates from the back of this book. There are several ways to transfer those images to your material. Each project will detail which technique works best, but here are our most-used options.

Graphite transfer To use this technique, rub the back of a printed image with a thick, dark layer of graphite. Tape the image face up to your linoleum block or other surface, and trace the image. A faint outline will be left behind on your surface, which you can then cut, carve, or ink.

Transfer paper Similar to the graphite transfer option, you can use a sheet of transfer paper between your printed image and your surface. The transfer paper acts as the graphite layer. Tape the transfer paper and then the printed image on top of your carving or printing surface, and trace the outline with a pen or pencil.

Tracing If you can see through your surface (for example, if you are printing on plastic or glass), then you will simply be tracing an image directly on your material. Place the printed image behind your surface and trace it. Fill it in with ink, or paint it with ink and a stencil brush.

STAMP CARVING

Before cutting directly into your stamp block, make some practice cuts on the material you intend to carve. Use different sizes of carver tips to become more comfortable with the materials before you start your project. You can always take more material away, but you can't fill in linoleum, rubber, or cork that has been carved out, so cut carefully and slowly.

Linoleum blocks are made from linseed oil, cork, and resin. It will dry out over time, so it is best to use fresh blocks before they harden and crack. Once a linoleum block is carved and saturated with ink, it will last much longer. If you do have a tough block, either by the nature of the material or from being dried out over time, you can warm up the surface with an iron on a low setting. This will make it easier to carve. Also, we often use a synthetic, rubberlike block of material called E-Z-Cut that is thicker and easier to carve through than traditional linoleum.

* Don't forget that carved images will print in reverse, so make sure any text or directional images are transferred in reverse.

* Whether you are cutting into rubber, linoleum, or cork, always carve away from your hand and on a nonslip surface for safety. Block cutters and blades are very sharp!

* Be mindful to turn the block in different directions as you work; otherwise, you will have the tendency to twist your body instead.

You can mount your linoleum block stamps to a block of wood when you are finished, which will give your hand or brayer a stable base to hold and press. Choose a silicon adhesive that is water resistant and will bond to both wood and rubber/vinyl. Goop® Adhesive has those characteristics and also dries flexible, so it won't crack under pressure.

STAMPING TIPS

Once you've got a design carved, you'll need to choose your ink and get ready to stamp.

* If you are using a tube or pot of ink, pour a dollop at a time onto an acrylic plate or other smooth surface and spread it with a brayer. Dip your stamp into the spread ink or use the brayer to roll an even layer onto the stamp. If you are using a stamp pad, you can blot directly into the ink.

* When inking up a stamp, dab into the ink several times and test it for even coverage on scrap paper or fabric.

* When you make contact with the paper or fabric surface, aim for a single movement and press down firmly. Do not rock the stamp or your hand back and forth, as it will blur your lines. If the surface area is too big, place the stamp down gently and roll the brayer on top for even pressure.

* Lift the stamp quickly, upward and away from the work to avoid smudging.

* Always let the ink dry completely. This usually takes longer than you think it should! Try not to touch the image before it's dry. You will heat-set most ink on fabric with an iron on a low setting.

INK OPTIONS

Dye-based ink Acid-free, fade resistant, permanent, and smearproof when dry, dye-based inks are made to heat-set on regular or glossy paper, glass, plastic, acrylic, or metal. Hero Arts® Neon brand has some of the best bright colors we've seen in dye-based ink pads.

Pigment pads Known for very bright and opaque colors, pigment ink is thicker than dye-based ink and therefore slower to dry. Pigment ink will dry on any uncoated surface, since it requires absorption on the surface. Heat-setting it will speed the drying time and set it permanently to fabric. ColorBox® brand is among our favorite pigment-based ink pads.

Textile ink Jacquard brand textile color is our favorite, because it is the most versatile and easy to use. It is colorfast, semi-opaque, and washable, and you can apply it directly to natural or synthetic materials. This ink can be applied with a sponge, brush, roller, or stamps.

Porcelain paint pens Pebeo Porcelaine Paint pens are a great option for inking the surface of glass, ceramic, or porcelain. Baking the project in an oven helps set the paint, but this brand will cure without baking and is still wash resistant.

Permanent markers The ink in permanent markers works great on more than just paper. Brands such as Sharpie®, Le Pen, and Micron® have incredibly fine-point markers in a huge array of colors that work on fabric, ceramic, and glass.

CARING FOR STAMPS AND INK

Stamps and ink can last for quite a while if you take proper care of them.

To prevent your ink pads from getting muddy, clean your stamps thoroughly every time you change colors. Store ink pads level and upside down. This prevents uneven ink distribution and keeps the surface fully inked.

Stamps can be cleaned using a bottle of stamp cleaner or an all-purpose household cleaning solution. Avoid oil-based cleaners, which can deteriorate the material. Apply the cleaner directly to the stamp, and wipe it off with a sponge. Blot the stamp dry with a paper towel. Alcohol-free baby wipes work well, too. These cleaning solutions will work for rubber, linoleum, synthetic blocks, and cork. However, you will want to be extra gentle with rubber and cork, which crumble easily when rubbed.

TIPS AND ADVICE FOR PROJECTS USING WOOD AND STONE

Wood and stone make beautiful projects and accents. Their natural irregularities can have unexpected effects. The following tips are to encourage you to explore these materials with confidence.

CHOOSING WOOD MATERIALS

Our projects use a variety of sticks and tree-based bits. Feel free to substitute what you can source most easily.

Poplar This is our wood of choice for the **Poplar Nesting Boxes** on p.56 for several reasons. It is one of the softest hardwoods available, making it easy to saw through and nail. Poplar also is considered by many to be one of the best woods to paint and is naturally resistant to decay.

TIPS FOR WORKING WITH WOOD AND STONE

* Be sure to gently sand the project wood, then wipe it with a damp cloth and let it dry before it's painted or glued.

* You can leave unpainted areas natural. Or seal the wood by staining/varnishing it.

* Keep your wood projects free of moisture.

* A handsaw will work for trimming wood to size, but an electric one makes the job easier.

* Wash stones in warm, soapy water, and let them dry completely before painting or gluing them.

* If you are using found rocks that have a variety of textures, the paint or images added to the surface will vary as well.

THE
PROJECTS

BLOCK-PRINTED FUROSHIKI WRAP

DIFFICULTY
LEVEL

Furoshiki refers to a Japanese cloth used to wrap and carry gifts, groceries, or anything that might require an extra hand or two. This DIY version is a great way to personalize your parcel, and it makes a reusable and eco-friendly alternative to wrapping paper and plastic or paper bags.

MATERIALS

* 24-in. lightweight, solid cotton fabric square
* Approx. 1 yard scrap yarn, any color
* Fabric-friendly ink pad
* Thread in a coordinating color

TOOLS

* Small wood block, any size, that suits your intended pattern
* Masking tape
* 24-in. by 24-in. (or larger) cardboard sheet
* Scrap paper

WHAT WE USED

* Robert Kaufman Chambray Union Light Indigo fabric
* 1½-in. square wood block
* ColorBox crafter's ink in Snow

Instructions

MAKE THE BLOCK STAMP

1. Tape one end of the yarn to the back of the block of wood. Wrap the yarn tightly around the block in any direction you like, and tape the finishing end on the back as well.

Note: We chose to wrap the yarn in one direction, but you can overlap or crisscross it to create any pattern.

2. Test the block on paper before you stamp onto the material. You can also test the stamp on some of the fabric, if you have extra, to make sure you are happy with the design.

STAMP THE FABRIC

3. Adhere the fabric to a piece of cardboard by taping the perimeter in about ¼ in. on all sides. Since the fabric is on the thin side, the ink will bleed through to the back, and the cardboard will absorb the extra ink while also keeping the work surface flat.

4. Load the stamp with ink by dabbing it on the ink pad. Starting in one corner of the fabric and working in rows, stamp the design. You can alternate the direction of the stamp, as we did, or even overlap layers. Calculate the layout of the design before you begin, or stamp randomly as you go.

(Continued)

5. Let the ink dry completely. Remove the tape holding the fabric to the cardboard. Iron the back side of the fabric on a low setting to set the ink.

FINISH THE FABRIC

6. Iron a ¼-in. hem around all four sides of the fabric. Turn the ironed hem over itself another ¼ in. to tuck the raw edges under. Pin it in place, and sew around the entire perimeter of the fabric using a straight stitch. Ironing the seams before pinning the hem in place will give you a crisp edge to sew over.

WRAP THE PARCEL

7. Start with the box (our box measured 6 in. by 6 in. by 3 in.) in the center of the fabric, turning the box at a 45-degree angle. Bring the first corner up and over the box. Tuck the flap either under the box or under itself.

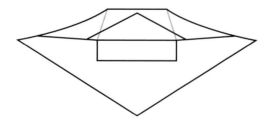

8. Bring the opposite corner over the tucked fabric, and let the corner hang off of the top side of the box.

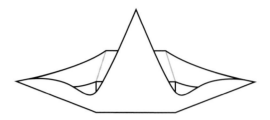

9. Bring the other two opposing corners over the top.

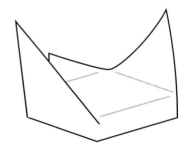

10. Tie them in a square knot.

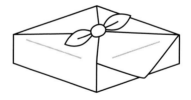

WOODEN BAUBLE NECKLACE

DIFFICULTY
LEVEL

Remember stringing macaroni necklaces as a kid? Well, this project is just as easy but a little more fashion-forward! It's easy to create this necklace by using a bit of paint and some wooden beads. You can follow our instructions exactly, or you can remove, swap out, or add beads and extra colors for a unique touch. Change it up depending on your mood or outfit.

MATERIALS

* 9 round wooden beads, ½ in. diameter
* Acrylic paint, 3 colors
* Washi tape or painter's tape
* Gold chain with clasp

TOOLS

* Wood glue or strong glue of your choice
* Sponge brush
* Twine

WHAT WE USED

* Galeria Acrylic Paint in Cadmium Red Light and White
* Craft Essentials Acrylic Paint in Aqua

Instructions

1. Wrap washi tape or painter's tape completely around one-half of each bead, making a straight line in the middle. Be sure the line wraps around the "belly" of the bead, with the holes centered top and bottom.

2. Paint the exposed half in acrylic paint with a sponge brush, in sets of three beads per color. You may want to apply two coats of paint for even coverage. Let the paint dry completely.

3. String two beads of each color onto scrap twine, with the matching colored halves touching each other. Apply glue to the point where the two colored beads meet, and press them together.

4. Lay the string of beads on a table, and hold the third bead in the trio up to the pair on the string to see where the painted sides meet. Apply glue to those two points on the third bead, where it touches the other two in its family. Hold the third bead in place until set. Repeat attaching the third bead for the other two color sets.

5. Remove the three trios from the twine and string onto a gold chain of your choosing.

SCANDINAVIAN MINI BLANKET

DIFFICULTY
LEVEL

Here in Seattle, we celebrate Nordic heritage in a big way. Immigrants from Norway, Sweden, Finland, Denmark, and Iceland settled in the Pacific Northwest long ago and were once the largest ethnic group in Washington. We wanted to honor that heritage with this chic baby blanket that sports the Scandinavian cross: a nod to each nation's flag. The black and white color scheme attracts newborns' eyes and looks great with any décor.

MATERIALS

* 1 yard white or cream flannel
* 2¼-in. by 2¼-in. linoleum block
* Black fabric ink (non-toxic)
* Thread to match flannel
* Muslin or scrap fabric

TOOLS

* Precision knife
* Graphite pencil
* Acrylic ruler
* Rotary cutter
* Iron
* Sewing machine with an edging stitch
* Kraft paper (or other protective table covering)
* Tape or pins
* Ink brayer
* Cross Stamp template (p. 81)

WHAT WE USED

* Robert Kaufman Flannel Solid in Snow
* Jaquard Black Textile Ink

Instructions

MAKE THE CROSS STAMP

1. Photocopy the Cross Stamp template. Rub the back side of the photocopy image with a graphite pencil. Make sure you cover the area behind the outline well—holding the sheet up to a light source can help ensure you have fulled covered the template.

2. Tape the template onto the surface of the linoleum block, graphite side down. Trace the outline of the design with a pencil. This will transfer a faint line of graphite in the shape of the design onto the linoleum block.

3. Use the precision knife to cut along the outline of the cross, removing the excess pieces. Since this image is all straight lines, you don't need to carve the stamp using a linocut tool.

MAKE THE BLANKET

4. Wash, dry, and iron the flannel. Use a rotary cutter and ruler to cut the fabric to a 32-in. square.

5. Lay the kraft paper or other protective covering over your workspace, since the ink can sometimes soak through the fabric and get messy. Tape or pin the fabric in place.

6. Ink up the stamp using the brayer and fabric ink. Practice a few times on a scrap of the same fabric to test the amount of ink you will need for a good impression. Using the diagram

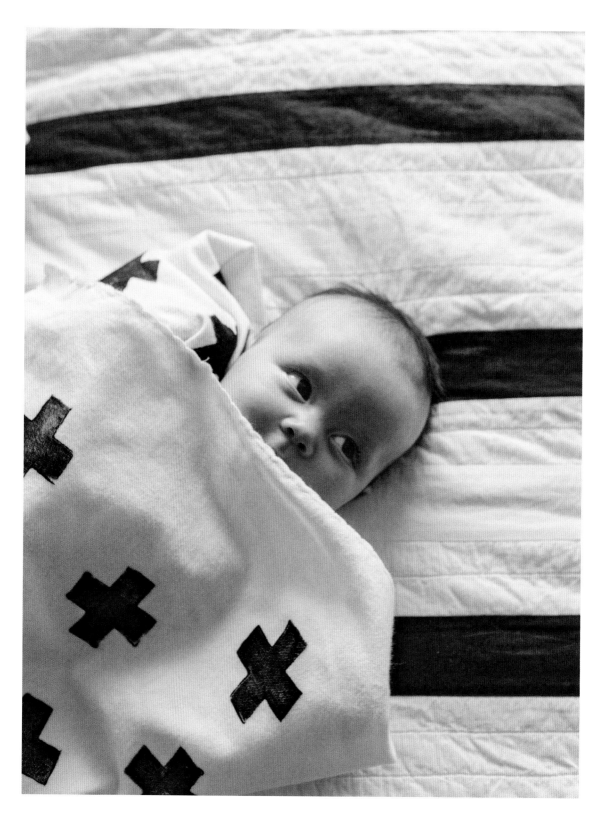

EVEN SPACING

If you choose to calculate the spacing, use a ruler to measure the center point of each stamp. Then start with the center row and make small pencil marks where each cross will fall. Continue marking and stamping the rows, with each cross equidistant from the other. There should be about 1¾ in. between each stamp.

below as a guide, map out where the crosses will be stamped. You will have seven rows overall—four rows of seven and three rows of six. You can definitely eyeball the placement of the crosses, accounting for a 3-in. border around the entire blanket.

7. When you have completed the stamping, allow the fabric to dry for 24 to 48 hours depending on the ink's instructions.

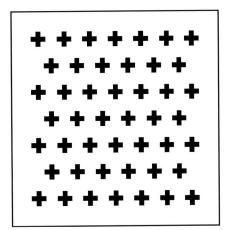

8. Place the piece of scrap muslin or fabric over the top of the design. With the iron on its lowest setting, heat-set the fabric ink by gently pressing the iron onto the muslin. Hold it for about 5 seconds, then set another area, continuing until the entire blanket design has been set. Refer to the textile ink packaging for any other specific setting instructions.

9. Complete the blanket with a sweet finishing touch by using any border stitch on your sewing machine with a ⅛-in. or ¼-in. allowance around the edge. Zigzag or scallop stitches work well. Or you can also choose to hand-sew a cross blanket stitch (p. 13) or a long and short stitch (p. 13) around the border.

INK SAFETY

If you are planning to make this blanket for an infant or young child, like we did, be sure to use a food-grade, non-toxic ink. Babies often put things in their mouth, and it is always better to be safe!

FRUIT & VEGGIE
DIP-DYE SWATCHES

DIFFICULTY
LEVEL

Homemade dyes always seemed like so much fun. However, being the purists that we are, we needed to do some serious experiments before we felt ready to dunk our crisp white linens into a vegetable bath. The results of using natural ingredients were beautiful and subtle, reminiscent of watercolor painting, and we couldn't help but fall in love with the process. Here are our not-so-scientific findings! You can see the dying technique put into practice in our **Stenciled Cocktail Napkins** project on p. 39.

MATERIALS

* 4-in. by 6-in. pieces of white cotton twill fabric (or any natural, undyed fibers such as silk or linen)
* Fruits and veggies
* Distilled white vinegar (for veggie dyes)
* Kosher salt (for fruit dyes)

TOOLS

* Medium pot, 1 per dye
* Small glass jar with lid, 1 per dye
* Fine strainer

WHAT WE USED

* Strawberries, blueberries, red beets, yellow and red onion skins, spinach, purple cabbage, and paprika

Instructions

PREPARE THE DYE

1. Chop the chosen ingredients into very fine bits. The chart on p. 32 offers some possible dyes, but you can also experiment with other fruits, vegetables, and spices.

2. Put one part ingredient into a pot with two parts water. For example, 1 cup of strawberry bits requires 2 cups of water. Bring the mixture to a boil, and simmer it for one hour.

Note: After about an hour, the ingredients will have released most of their color and the water will have reduced slightly.

3. Strain all of the bits out of the dye. Place the dye into a jar to cool.

(Continued)

FIXATIVES

* For a fruit dye fixative: Combine ¼ cup of salt per 4 cups of water.

* For a veggie dye fixative: Combine 1 cup of vinegar per 4 cups of water.

TIP

Keep in mind that a lot of the vibrancy will be lost when the fabric is rinsed for the first time. This is normal. Some ingredients keep saturation better than others. For example, the blueberry we used kept a stronger color than the red beets when washed, even though both dyes were equally rich in color. After a wash or two, the color should remain consistent thereafter. We recommend you wash any dyed fabrics separately the first few times so that the colors do not bleed into undyed fabrics. You can always re-dye your fabric to revive the color, as well.

PREPARE THE FABRIC

4. For the dye to adhere to the fabric, you'll need to create a fixative. Boil your fabric in the appropriate fixative for one hour (see p. 30 and below).

5. After an hour, rinse the fabric in cool water. It is now ready to dye.

DYE THE FABRIC

6. Place the wet fabric directly into the dye. Let it sit for as long as you like—our swatches soaked for 24 hours. The longer the fabric sits, the stronger the dye color.

Note: We only dipped half of the fabric into the dye and let the rest hang outside of the jar for comparison. Each of the colors created some degree of variation—some dyes quickly crept up the fabric swatch, and some dyes fixed only where the fabric was in direct contact with the dye.

7. When you are happy with the saturation, remove the fabric from the dye and rinse it in cold water; let dry.

Dyes to Try

INGREDIENT	FIXATIVE	FINISHED COLOR
COFFEE	VINEGAR & WATER	BROWN
PAPRIKA	VINEGAR & WATER	PALE ORANGE
TURMERIC	VINEGAR & WATER	YELLOW
SPINACH	VINEGAR & WATER	GREEN
RED & YELLOW ONION SKIN	VINEGAR & WATER	RUST
BEET	VINEGAR & WATER	PALE PINK
STRAWBERRY	SALT & WATER	PINK
RED CABBAGE	VINEGAR & WATER	ICY BLUE
BLUEBERRY	SALT & WATER	DEEP PURPLE

> Above, swatches from left to right: Paprika, spinach, red and yellow onion skin, beet, strawberry, purple cabbage, and blueberry.

SKETCHED
SALT & PEPPER JARS

DIFFICULTY
LEVEL

Create a charming contrast of black and white against salt and pepper with these tiny tabletop staples. These little cuties would be adorable filled with cinnamon and sugar, too. Attach a set of demi spoons and you've got a great thank-you, hostess, or housewarming present.

MATERIALS

* 2.7-oz. Weck canning jars, set of 2

TOOLS

* Scissors
* Tape
* Fine-tip black porcelain paint pen
* Fine-tip white porcelain paint pen
* Sketched Salt & Pepper Jars pattern (p. 81)

Instructions

1. Photocopy the Sketched Salt & Pepper Jars pattern.

2. Cut out the pattern and place it inside one of the jars. Center the paper and tape it in place so the pattern is seamless. The jar's interior is slightly tapered, so the paper will naturally bend. If you tape it in two or more places, the pattern should line up well.

3. Use the porcelain paint pen to trace the pattern on the exterior wall. Sketch one jar in white ink and one in black ink.

4. Let the ink dry for 24 hours and, if indicated on the pen's package directions, bake the jars in the oven at the appropriate temperature to set the ink.

5. Fill the jars with the spices of your choosing.

TIPS

* The thickness of the glass wall creates distance between the pattern design and surface area. Your sketch may seem off the mark at first, but once you get going, the design should transfer correctly.

* Weck jars have their classic logo embossed on the side wall of their jars. Just paint right over them!

CORK-STAMPED WRAPPING PAPER

DIFFICULTY
LEVEL

What goes better with crafts than wine? This is a simple project that relies on using recycled materials and basic tools. Have some friends over to help you polish off a few bottles (with cheese, please!) and then get to work creating your own cork stamps and wrapping paper. You can even create custom wine bottle labels to gift to friends, so they can begin their own stamp collection.

MATERIALS

* Several wine corks (made of cork, not plastic)
* Solid-colored wrapping paper or kraft paper

TOOLS

* Precision knife
* Ink pads
* Pencil
* Scrap paper

WHAT WE USED

* 30-in. by 10-ft. Paper Source® solid color wrapping paper roll in Ecowhite
* Hero Arts Neon ink pads in Pink and Orange
* ColorBox ink pads in Black and Ocean

Instructions

1. Draw a design onto the flat end of a wine cork (the side that does not have the hole made by the corkscrew) with a pencil.

2. Using the precision knife, gently cut away the negative space of the stamp's design. Cut into the cork about ¼ in., and slowly slice away any material that is left behind.

Note: Cork can sometimes be crumbly—do your best to create straight lines, but remember that this project is intended to look natural and handmade.

3. After you have removed all of the negative space, ink up the stamp using a dye or pigment ink pad and stamp several practice impressions on a scrap piece of paper. The impressions will look better the more you use the stamp, as the cork will absorb ink and make a fuller impression. If you aren't happy with the impression as it is, trim away additional cork as you see fit to better shape the design.

4. To create the wrapping paper, first choose the stamp designs and color scheme. Ink up the stamps and gently press them onto the wrapping paper or kraft paper. Allow the ink to dry completely before wrapping the gift or bottle.

(Continued)

TIPS

* Champagne corks are great for this project because they don't require a corkscrew to remove.

* Simple shapes make the best impressions (like a starburst, a tiny house, or a heart).

* If you are drawing letters, make sure that you draw a reverse image of the letter, as the stamp impression will print backwards.

* To clean your stamps, soak them in a bowl of water overnight, and use a bit of household cleaning spray to remove excess ink into a paper towel. Allow them to dry completely.

STENCILED COCKTAIL NAPKINS

Whether you are throwing a swanky cocktail party for a crowd or simply enjoying a game night for two, these napkins fit the bill. The stencil pattern is graphic but minimal, making it an easy piece to cut and print a few times or many. Best of all, you can use these napkins again and again, throwing one in with your weekday lunch, packing a few for an impromptu pic-nic, and keeping a stack with your bar accessories.

MATERIALS

* 10-in. fabric cocktail napkin set
* 12-in. by 12-in. blank stencil sheet
* Textile ink

TOOLS

* Pencil
* Metal ruler
* Precision knife
* Masking tape
* Thick cardboard work surface (any size larger than your napkins)
* ½-in. round stipple brush
* Iron
* Scrap paper or fabric
* Stenciled Cocktail Napkins template (p. 82)

Instructions

PREPARE THE NAPKINS

1. Begin with napkins that are washed, dried, and ironed. We used a set of premade white cotton napkins and dip-dyed them with strawberries using the technique from **Fruit & Veggie Dip-Dye Swatches** (p. 30).

2. Tape the corners of one napkin to a piece of cardboard or another similarly flat work surface that can absorb any ink that bleeds through.

(Continued)

PREPARE THE STENCIL

3. Photocopy the Stenciled Cocktail Napkins template.

4. Tape the stencil template, right side up, to the back of the stencil sheet. Then trace the arrow and line pattern with a pencil. Use a ruler for straighter edges.

5. Use the precision knife and ruler to cut the drawn arrows and lines away from the main stencil sheet.

PRINTING THE NAPKINS

6. Center and place the cut stencil sheet over the napkin that is attached to the cardboard. Tape it to the cardboard as shown at right.

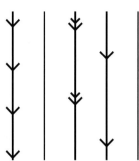

7. Dip the stipple brush into the textile ink. Blot off the excess on scrap paper or fabric.

8. Gently dab the brush over the stencil pattern, making contact with the napkin. For cleaner lines, it is better to dab and dot in an up-and-down motion, instead of swiping or gliding the brush over the stencil.

9. When the entire pattern is covered with ink, gently lift the stencil away from the napkin and cardboard work surface. Carefully remove the napkin from the cardboard work surface, and set it aside to dry completely.

10. Tape another napkin to the work surface, and repeat the stenciling process beginning from step 6. Be sure there is no ink on the back side of the stencil before using it again.

FINISHING

11. When the ink on all of the printed napkins is completely dry, iron the napkin to set the ink. Place a piece of scrap fabric over the design. With the iron on its lowest setting, heat-set the textile paint by gently pressing the iron onto the fabric. Hold it for about 5 seconds, then set another area. Continue until the entire design has been set. Refer to the textile ink packaging for any other specific setting instructions.

SIMPLE
FELT PLACEMATS

This is an easy project for anyone who appreciates minimalist design and a clean aesthetic. All it takes is some colored felt and a bit of textile paint to create a bold pattern that fits right in to a modern tablescape. The cooking, however, is entirely up to you—we can't help you there.

MATERIALS

Note: Each felt piece will make one placemat.

* **12-in. by 18-in. felt, 3mm thick**
* **Black textile ink**
* **Muslin or scrap fabric**

TOOLS

* **Scissors or rotary cutter**
* **Stippling sponge or brush**
* **Small round drinking glass, 2¾ in. diameter**
* **Pencil (or tailor's chalk)**
* **Iron**

WHAT WE USED

* **3mm wool felt in Salmon, Mustard, and Aqua Mist**
* **Jaquard textile ink in Black**

Instructions

1. Place the glass on top of the back side of the felt, open side down, just touching the two edges at the corner of the felt. Use the tailor's chalk or pencil to trace around the outer edge of the glass to give the felt a rounded outer corner. Repeat in all the corners of the felt, making sure to position the glass so that the curve is the same on each corner. After tracing the curves, use scissors or the rotary cutter to carefully trim the corners.

2. To create the pattern on the felt, dip the stippling sponge or brush into the textile paint, and sponge off the excess into a paper towel. Use the sponge or brush to create patterns of polka dots, swishes, or short lines.

Note: Practice making patterns with the textile paint on inexpensive acrylic felt. That way, if you make a mistake you won't waste your 3mm-thick felt.

3. Allow the paint to dry for 24 hours (or follow the instructions on the ink container).

4. Place the piece of muslin or scrap fabric over the top of the design. With the iron on its lowest setting, heat-set the textile paint by gently pressing the iron onto the muslin. Hold it for about 5 seconds, then set another area, continuing until the entire placemat design has been set. Refer to the textile ink packaging for any other specific setting instructions.

TEENY, TINY
ERASER STAMPS

DIFFICULTY
LEVEL

Let's face it. Pretty much anything in miniature size is adorable—Chihuahuas, babies, dollhouse kitchen accessories, and especially rubber stamps. These teeny, tiny eraser stamps are fun to make and use or give away. This is a great exercise in stamp making and can get the creative process flowing for larger-scale projects such as the **Honeycomb Linoleum Block Stamps** on p. 47.

MATERIALS

* **Pencils with rubber eraser tops**
* **Scrap paper**

TOOLS

* **Pen**
* **Precision knife**
* **Ink pad**

Instructions

1. Sketch out some simple shapes on scrap paper. We made arrow, heart, cross, triangle, and line designs.

2. Copy the designs you choose onto the eraser tops using a pen.

3. Carefully trace the lines with a precision knife. Then start carving away the negative space from the edges of the design. On a traditional pencil eraser, carve about ⅛ in. deep because you'll want to keep as much stability as possible. If you make a mistake, just cut off the top layer of the eraser and start again.

(Continued)

TIPS

* When cutting a small surface, the more basic the shape is, the better.

* Straight lines are easier to carve than curved lines.

* Shapes that extend to the edge of the eraser are easier to carve than shapes that leave a border.

* Decide what parts of the shape will remain and what parts are carved away before you begin to cut.

* Remember that anything directional (for example, a number or initial) will print in reverse.

* Use small, shallow cuts. You can always remove more eraser, but you can't put it back.

Note: You'll be working the blade very close to your fingers, so use caution with your precision knife.

4. Try stamping the work-in-progress on scrap paper. You'll see the results clearly and can keep carving to perfect your shapes.

WAYS TO USE THEM

* Make a gift! Tie a handful of pencils together and put them in a mug, jar, or pencil case with a mini ink pad.

* Carve an X and an O. Make a tiny tic-tac-toe game. Or stamp all of your letters with hugs and kisses.

* Carve the whole alphabet or digits 0 to 9. Little kids would have a blast stamping with the eraser side (with washable ink!) and then practice tracing their numbers and letters with the pencil side.

* Use these little stamps to decorate cards, small gift packages, and stationery.

HONEYCOMB LINOLEUM BLOCK STAMPS

Using linoleum to carve your own stamp is fun and easy! You can turn almost any design into a hand-carved image to use on paper or fabric. Starting with our simple honeycomb shape is a great way to learn how to carve, and then you can use the same techniques to create one-of-a-kind artwork. Try using this stamp to embellish the **Japanese Stab Bound Guest Book** (p. 78).

MATERIALS

* 4-in. by 6-in. unmounted, soft linoleum carving block
* Ink pad

TOOLS

* Graphite pencil
* Scrap paper
* Tape
* Lino cutter handle with a variety of nibs (at least one fine and one large gouge)
* Precision knife
* Honeycomb Linoleum Block Stamps template (p. 83)

WHAT WE USED

* MOO Carve Printing Block
* Speedball cutter with no. 1, no. 2, and no. 5 blades

Instructions

1. Photocopy the Honeycomb Linoleum Block Stamps template. Rub the back side of the photocopied image with a graphite pencil. Make sure you cover the area behind the outline well—holding the sheet up to a light source can help.

2. Tape the template onto the surface of the linoleum block, graphite side down. Trace the outline of the design with a pencil. This will transfer a faint line of graphite in the shape of the design onto the linoleum block.

(Continued)

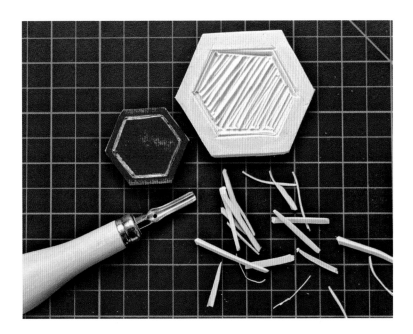

3. If you are creating your own image and aren't happy with the transfer, you can erase the marks from the block or even draw directly onto the block. Remember that the stamped image will be printed in reverse, so be sure any text or directional images are first drawn mirrored. Keep in mind what parts of the image will be recessed, creating negative space.

4. To begin carving, insert the thinnest blade into the lino cutter. Gently glide the cutter along the outline of the shape. Always push the cutter away from you, and be careful as you brace the block with your other hand. You should see a very thin strip of linoleum removed with each cut.

Note: It is best to start with shallow cuts because you'll have more control with the cutting tool. If you start your cuts too deep, you may make gouges that rip apart the block surface.

5. As you continue to work around the outline, you can switch to a larger blade to remove more linoleum with each pass. At any point in the carving process, you can ink up the block and stamp it on scrap paper to see how the design is progressing and to identify which spots need more work. If the edges of the piece are straight, such as with these honeycombs, you can completely cut off the corners of the block so the entire stamp is the outlined shape.

6. When you are happy with the finished carving, stamp away!

INK OR PAINT TO MAKE MORE THINGS!

Once your stamp is made, you can use it with traditional stamp pads on both paper and fabric surfaces (most brands list appropriate ones). You can paint your stamping surface with acrylic paint and a paint or sponge brush. Or you can use block printing ink, but be sure to find one specifically suited to your surface material. Each type of ink and surface will create a new dimension to your printed image, so have fun experimenting.

STAMPED & EMBROIDERED HONEYCOMB TABLE RUNNER

DIFFICULTY LEVEL

Multidimensional projects like this one are the most interesting and fun to tackle. We designed this runner to incorporate block printing, embroidery, *and* machine sewing. Each individual skill is not too difficult, and when combined, they create a special table linen with a fresh honeycomb motif. Simple place settings and neutral-toned accessories allow the eye-catching embroidery to be the showcase of the table. Style it up with gold flatware and an antique goblet or two and you've got yourself a dinner party!

MATERIALS

* White linen, 2 yards (washed, dried, and ironed)
* White thread
* Embroidery floss in a variety of colors

TOOLS

* Stamping ink
* Scissors
* 6-in. embroidery hoop
* Embroidery needle
* Large Honeycomb Linoleum Block Stamp (p. 47)

WHAT WE USED

* Robert Kaufman Antwerp Linen White fabric
* Brilliance Galaxy Gold ink pad
* DMC® embroidery floss 606 (Red-orange), 351 (Coral), 353 (Light Pink-coral), 892 (Hot Pink), 543 (Pale Salmon), 3970 (Taupe), 729 (Gold), and White

Instructions

1. Cut two pieces of fabric 15 in. wide by 47 in. long.

2. Using the large Honeycomb Linoleum Block Stamp, create a design on one of the pieces of fabric. We made a cascading pattern with the larger honeycomb shape in a very light gold ink.

3. Put the stamped fabric into an embroidery hoop, centering the honeycomb with which you wish to start. Tighten the hoop, keeping the fabric taut.

4. Thread the embroidery needle with a workable length of floss, and knot the end. Begin by pushing your needle up from the

USING A DIFFERENT STAMP

You can use a different stamp if you like, but keep in mind that you'll be using an embroidery stitch called the satin stitch. This works best to fill larger blocks of color and is not ideal for small, detailed, or thin-lined images. The satin stitch will cover most of the stamped image, but some ink color may peek through the edges. Take that into account when choosing your ink and embroidery floss colors.

TIP

As you work the satin stitch around the corners of the honeycomb, your stitches may start to fan out or become slightly angled. You can either straighten out as you reach a straighter area, or begin making stitches at a slight angle when you start. If you need more floss, knot it at the back side and start a new piece where you left off. Knot and tie off when you reach the end.

back to the front of the work at any point along the border of the image. Use the satin stitch (p. 14) to cover the entire stamped image.

5. Loosen the hoop, and adjust the fabric to center on another stamped image. Continue with the satin stitching for the entire piece, changing colors as often as you like. You can keep some of the stamped images unembroidered, too. Or you can embroider with white floss on the white linen for an interesting and subtle effect.

6. When the fabric is embroidered to your liking, remove it from the hoop and iron it flat.

7. Pin the other piece of fabric to the embroidered piece, right sides together. Sew the two layers together with a ¼-in. seam allowance, making sure to leave a 3-in. gap open at one of the ends. To remove excess bulk, trim the corners of the fabric, being careful not to snip your threads.

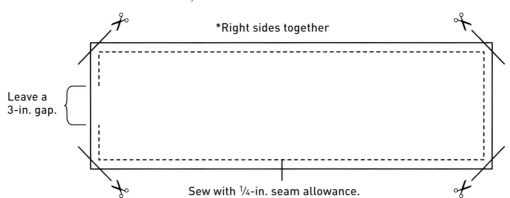

*Right sides together

Leave a 3-in. gap.

Sew with ¼-in. seam allowance.

8. Pull the entire piece right side out through the 3-in. opening. Work the corners to a point. Flip the seam allowance from the 3-in. opening into the work and pin in place. Iron the entire work flat. Topstitch a ¼-in. border around the perimeter of the work, making sure to sew over and close the 3-in. gap.

MATCHBOX CONFETTI BOXES

If you don't have a party planned already, you will want to get the ball rolling! These confetti boxes are so fun and festive—we can't think of an event for which they wouldn't be perfect. Birthday parties, baby or bridal showers, or a Fourth of July or New Year's Eve celebration would all be even more exciting with these confetti boxes. Don't sneeze!

MATERIALS

* 1 sheet of cardstock per box
* Several sheets of colorful paper
* Stamps and ink or other decorative embellishments

TOOLS

* Pencil
* Scissors
* Straightedge ruler
* Bone folder (optional)
* Double-sided tape or glue
* Round or triangle hole punch
* Matchbox Confetti Boxes template (p. 84)

WHAT WE USED

* Canford Cardstock in Ice White
* ColorBox stamp pad in Black
* Teeny, Tiny Eraser Stamps (p. 44)
* Scotch® permanent double-sided tape, ¼ in. wide

Instructions

1. Photocopy and cut out the Matchbox Confetti Boxes template. There are two pieces per box: an inner tray and an outer wrap. Trace and cut as many matchbox pieces as you need from cardstock.

2. Assemble the inner tray piece. Fold the cardstock at each of the dotted lines. For extra-crisp lines, score it with a straight-edge and a bone folder, and run the bone folder over each of the creases. You can also use your thumb.

3. Apply glue or tape to each of the tabs. Fold up the long sides of the inner tray piece, and gently turn the tabs in toward the center. Then fold up the short sides of the box, and sandwich the tabs from the long sides between the short sides.

4. Make the outer wrap by scoring, folding, and creasing along each of the dotted lines. Fold this piece over the inner tray to make sure it fits snugly. Glue or tape along the last tab of the wrap and apply pressure to adhere.

5. Decorate and fill the boxes. Use the hole punch to punch out confetti from the colorful paper, and fill the boxes with the bits of punched paper. Decorate the boxes by gluing some of the punched paper to the outside of the boxes or by using the Teeny, Tiny Eraser Stamps.

POPLAR
NESTING BOXES

These boxes are minimalist in design, making them easy to incorporate into any setting. We adore the natural element of wood in our crafting and wanted to create a simple project that would be quick and easy for any level of crafter. These wooden boxes fill the bill—they are a cinch for a novice crafter to assemble. They consist of just four equal sides and a base that are nailed together —pretty simple and simply pretty!

MATERIALS

* ½-in.-thick wooden planks in the following sizes: 4 ft. by 3 in. for the tiny box, 4 ft. by 4 in. for the small box, 4 ft. by 6 in. for the medium box, and 4 ft. by 8 in. for the large box
* Acrylic paint, wood stain, and/or clear lacquer

TOOLS

* Hand, circular, or table saw
* Level
* Hammer and 1¼-in. finishing or casing nails, or a nail gun
* Sandpaper
* Paintbrush
* Painter's tape

WHAT WE USED

* Poplar wood planks, cut with a table saw
* 1¼-in. finishing nails
* Acrylic paint in Black, White, Gold, Turquoise, and Red-orange

Instructions

1. Begin with long planks of wood, one for each size box, that measure the correct width.

2. Measure and mark each piece needed per box along the plank, using the size chart below.

(Continued)

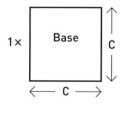

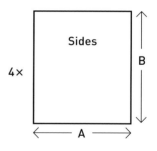

Nesting Box Plank Size Chart			
	SIDES (MAKE 4)		BASE (MAKE 1)
	A	B	C
TINY BOX	2 IN.	2½ IN.	1½ IN.
SMALL BOX	3 IN.	3½ IN.	2½ IN.
MEDIUM BOX	5 IN.	5½ IN.	4½ IN.
LARGE BOX	6¾ IN.	7¼ IN.	6¼ IN.

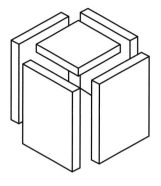

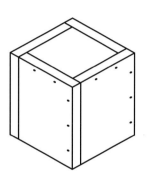

3. Cut the planks according to the marks. There should be five pieces per box—one base piece and four sides.

4. Place the base piece on a flat surface, and arrange each of the corresponding side pieces around its edges.

5. Clamp or tape the structure together, making sure all four sides are level and at right angles. Nail the sides to the base, with multiple nails along each edge to ensure sturdy construction. Sand any rough edges with sandpaper or a sanding block.

6. Repeat steps 3 to 5 for all four boxes.

7. Paint, stain, and/or lacquer the surfaces as you like. Use painter's tape to create sharp lines when color blocking.

TIP

Home improvement stores usually have a section of ¼-in. and ½-in. boards (poplar and cedar are common options) cut to standard widths and about 4 ft. long. You can begin with larger pieces of any wood you like, but the precut widths are helpful if you are trimming pieces by hand.

WAYS TO USE THEM

We designed these boxes to be multifunctional. They can be placed on any of their sides, with the open end face up or down, and they can be displayed individually or as a set. Best of all, they nest inside of each other to save space if you aren't using them all at once.

* With the open sides up, you can fill the boxes with trinkets or office supplies or use them as planters (don't plant directly in the box or the soil and moisture will rot the wood).

* With the closed base up, you can stack these boxes on a bookshelf or use them as risers for a display.

* On their sides, you can tuck toys inside or create mini dioramas.

SPIROGRAPHED TOTE

DIFFICULTY
LEVEL

If you are anything like us, then you probably had hours of fun playing with the Spirograph® as a kid. Only recently did we realize that the manufacturer was trying to teach us math; all we remember are bright colors and dizzying loops! You can re-create the fun with your littles by creating a Spirograph Tote for your books and pens. Grab your old (or find a new) Spirograph kit, and use our instructions for a more uniform look or create a free-form kaleidoscope of colors and shapes.

MATERIALS

- Medium-size canvas tote bag
- Fine-tip fabric markers in four colors

TOOLS

- Spirograph ring and wheel
- Removable mounting putty or tape
- Iron
- Paper or muslin
- Pencil

WHAT WE USED

- #52 Spirograph ring and wheel
- Le Pen markers in Dark Blue, Light Blue, Pink, and Orange
- Bag Works medium canvas tote (13½ in. by 13½ in. by 2 in.)

Instructions

1. Wash and iron the tote as per the manufacturer's instructions.

2. Decide the measurements or layout for the pattern. We made four columns and three rows of Spirograph designs, 8 full and 4 halves, for a total of 12. You can use a pencil to mark each center point, or cut 12 circles out of paper the size of the design and arrange them as you wish. For our tote, we started the first row 2¼ in. from the top and bottom and ¾ in. from the sides. Each design should be equidistant from each other in three clean rows.

3. After you have arranged the pattern, use putty or tape to secure the Spirograph ring to the tote bag to prevent movement.

4. Using the wheel (we used the second hole), begin making loops until the circle is complete. Continue in all of the spaces you have arranged for each Spirograph design.

5. For the "half" designs, simply complete half the number of loops. In our case, this was 52 of 105.

6. Alternate colors and wheels to create as many different patterns as you wish.

7. Allow the ink to dry completely. Place a sheet of paper or scrap of muslin over the inked parts. With the iron on its lowest setting, heat-set the ink by gently pressing the iron onto the muslin or paper. Hold it for about 5 seconds, then set another area, continuing until the entire design has been set.

PENS, PENCILS, WRITING UTENSILS

CHAMPION

CLOTHESPIN GARLAND

This garland is a new take on the old corkboard! The clothespins are visually fresh and interesting, and they're functional—holding notes, prints, or reminders. We hung this one above a desk space to clip inspirational illustrations and photos. Plus, it adds a pop of color to jump-start your creativity.

MATERIALS

* Old-fashioned wooden clothespins (about 100)
* Twine
* Acrylic paint, 2 colors

TOOLS

* Wood glue or strong glue of your choice
* Scissors
* Paintbrush or sponge brush

WHAT WE USED

* Honey-Can-Do DRY-01389 Traditional Wood Clothespins
* Acrylic paint in Golden Light Magenta
* Fine acrylic paint in Golden Iridescent Bright Gold

Instructions

1. Paint half of the clothespins one color and the other half another color. We recommend using two coats of paint for even coverage. Let the paint dry completely between coats and after applying the final coat.

2. Glue three clothespins of a single color together, rotating each clothespin slightly as shown below. Follow this procedure for all of the clothespins, working with sets of three clothespins at a time. Let the wood glue dry completely. Strong glue might dry much faster than wood glue so be careful not to glue your fingers together!

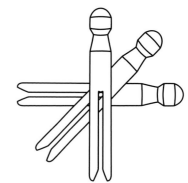

3. String all of the sets of clothespins along several yards of twine. We strung two trios of a single color and then alternated two trios of the second color, but you can try a number of patterns to find what suits you. Weave the twine through and around the joints as you string each one. You can leave space between each set, or make the garland one continuous strand of clothespins. Leave at least 6-in.-long twine tails at the start and end of the garland; you will use these tails for hanging the strand.

MINI ADVENTURE LOGS

Grab your bandana and a compass, and don't forget these Mini Adventure Logs! The Pacific Northwest has some of the most scenic and gorgeous trails in the country. Perfect for tracking your hike and collecting a few leaves, these pocket-size book-lets make taking notes convenient and stylish. Putting the pages together is quick using the pamphlet stitch, and it looks a lot cuter than a few side staples!

MATERIALS

Note: Makes one booklet.

* 5 sheets 8½-in. by 11-in. white text-weight paper
* 1 sheet 8½-in. by 5½-in. white cover-weight paper
* 12 in. string or twine

TOOLS

* Precision knife
* Bone folder (optional)
* Metal ruler or straightedge
* Pencil
* Embroidery needle
* Paper awl (optional)
* Black, red, and/or blue fine-tip markers
* Mini Adventure Logs Jig template (p. 85)
* Mini Adventure Logs Patterns (pp. 85–86)

Instructions

MAKE THE INTERIOR PAGES

1. Cut each of the 8½-in. by 11-in. sheets of text-weight paper in half so that you have 10 sheets of paper measuring 8½ in. by 5½ in. Fold each of these sheets of paper in half, creasing them with the bone folder or your thumbnail, to create the 20 interior pages of the book.

2. Nest the 10 folded sheets inside each other, creating a single signature.

MAKE THE HOLES

3. Photocopy and cut out the Mini Adventure Logs Jig template.

4. Place the jig inside the center fold of the booklet, placing the jig flush to the centerline. Make three marks with a pencil where the jig indicates.

(Continued)

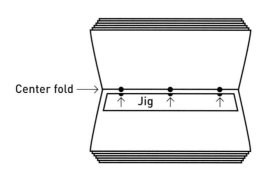

Center fold → | Jig

5. Using a paper awl or an embroidery needle, stab through the entire booklet of paper at each of the three marked points, poking from the inside out. If the 10 sheets are too thick to get through at once, split the booklet into two or more sections. Remember to nest all of the sheets back together and double-check that the holes line up.

6. Set the punched pages aside.

MAKE THE COVER

7. Using one of the plaid patterns on pp. 85–86, measure and mark the gridlines lightly using a ruler and pencil over the entire piece of cover-weight paper.

8. Once the grid is drawn, continue to follow the plaid pattern to fill in the colored areas with marker. We used thin diagonal lines to fill in our pattern, making sure the rows were slanted in one direction and columns were slanted in another so the lines would cross-hatch when overlapped.

9. Once the plaid pattern is filled in, you can erase the pencil grid, if you like.

10. Fold the cover in half, and crease it well with the bone folder or your thumbnail.

11. Use the Mini Adventure Logs Jig as you did in step 4 to mark and poke the three holes in the crease of the cover.

JOIN THE COVER TO THE INSIDE PAGES

12. Nest the interior pages into the cover sheet, lining up the holes at the spine. The pages and cover should be flush on the top and bottom. You will notice that the interior pages stick out beyond the right side of the cover. Use a ruler to measure how far the pages stick out—it is approximately ⅛ in., depending on how tightly the folds were creased at the start. Remove the interior pages from the cover, and use a straightedge or a ruler and a

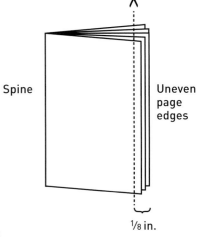

Spine

Uneven page edges

⅛ in.

precision knife to slice off that $\frac{1}{8}$ in. of excess paper. Place the sheets back into the cover to check that the entire booklet is now flush.

13. When you are sure that the sides are flush and the holes along the spine line up, sew the cover to the inside pages using the pamphlet stitch. Start by threading your needle with about 12 in. of twine. Enter the center hole from the outside of the spine, and push the needle into the center of the folded pages. Leave at least a 3-in. tail hanging out from the center hole. From the inside, exit out of the top hole, pushing the needle to the outside of the cover. Return the needle to the inside of the cover through the bottom hole on the outside, skipping the center hole. Exit through the center hole back to the starting point, and tie off with a knot. You can trim the tails close or leave them long enough to make a bow.

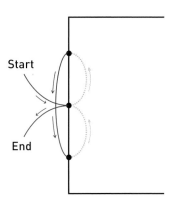

HOW TO USE THEM

These plaid covers are fun to make, but once you see how easy it is to make pamphlet books, you can decorate your covers in many ways. Try stamping your covers using the Teeny, Tiny Eraser Stamps from p. 44.

If you're not going on an outdoor adventure soon, consider using your booklets to track your reading list, record the funny things your kids say, take wine-tasting notes, or keep a dream journal.

CAMPFIRE STORYTELLING STONES

Camping is huge in the Pacific Northwest. In the summer, it seems like everyone is packing up their hybrid vehicles and heading for the hills, sleeping bags in tow. Whether you plan on toasting s'mores by the campfire or in your own backyard, you might want a game or two to play with your friends or kids. These Campfire Storytelling Stones are a great way to be creative and get ready for your summer holiday.

MATERIALS

* Found stones with a smooth surface
* Text-weight white paper

TOOLS

* White porcelain paint pen
* Black porcelain paint pen or Sharpie
* PVA adhesive
* Campfire Storytelling Stones templates (p. 87)

WHAT WE USED

* Found garden rocks
* Pebeo Porcelaine 150 Paint Marker in Anthracite Black
* Pebeo Porcelaine 150 Paint Marker in White
* Paper Source PVA adhesive

Instructions

1. Wash the stones in a bucket of soapy water. Rinse and dry them thoroughly.

2. Photocopy the Campfire Storytelling Stones templates onto sturdy, text-weight paper at a size that will fit onto the rocks you chose.

3. Color over the templates with a porcelain paint pen for a shiny finish. Use the black porcelain paint pen for the body of the image and the white for the details. Add any details that you wish. Cut out the templates. Use the pen along the edges of the cutout if there is any white space left by the scissors.

4. Glue the templates directly onto the rocks with PVA, and cover the rest of the rock with PVA for a shiny, "tumbled rock" look.

5. Allow the stones to dry completely, at least 24 hours.

(Continued)

WAYS TO USE THEM

- Randomly line up the stones, and have children create a story that introduces each element on the stones in order.

- Sit in a circle, and hand out one stone to each participant. Have one person start the story with a sentence that includes the image on his or her stone. The story moves to the next person in the circle, and he or she adds to the first person's plot by using the image on his or her stone.

- Flip the stones image side down. Take turns randomly choosing a stone and creating a storyline that way.

- Add a die to the game. Have participants take turns rolling the die and taking that many stones. Then have them create a single sentence using all of their chosen images.

- Create a game where one person poses a random camping-related "sticky situation." Another person randomly chooses a stone and has to imagine a solution involving his or her image. See how many ways you can escape an approaching bear or catch a fish without a pole!

PAINT-DIPPED BRANCH HOOKS

DIFFICULTY
LEVEL

Like the **Color-Blocked Stone Paperweights** (p. 74), this project is about bringing nature into your home. We encourage you to source your wood locally—as in your own backyard—if possible. Hooks like these are inspired by Scandinavian design and made with white birch. But you can experiment with different woods, shapes, and sizes to create a gallery of colorful, functional art in your home for hanging your jacket, towel, or jewelry.

MATERIALS

* Tree branch (1 in. to 2 in. diameter) with offshoots (1 in. to 5 in. diameter) that are each 4 in. to 5 in. long
* Acrylic paint in four colors of your choice
* Screws (and coordinating wall anchors)

TOOLS

* Table saw, reciprocating saw, or hand saw
* Carving knife
* Sandpaper
* Sponge brush
* Drill
* Safety gloves
* Painter's tape or washi tape
* Towel

WHAT WE USED

* Found branches
* Americana® Acrylic Paint in Spa Blue, Zinc, and Terra Coral
* Ceramcoat® Acrylic Paint in Yellow

Instructions

1. Remove the bark from the branch using the carving knife. Wear safety gloves to keep your fingers safe.

2. Select the sections of the branch that will become the area that is mounted to the wall. At roughly 4 in. to 6 in. long, these areas should have their own small branches attached to them (these smaller branches will act as the hook portion). Saw the entire piece off from the larger branch, then saw the offshoots (which will become the portion that you hang items on) to the desired length.

3. Saw vertically down the back of the branch's neck so that the branch now has a flat surface to place against the wall.

4. Locate a suitable spot in the branch for placing the screw that will mount the entire hook to the wall. Drill a hole in this spot that is compatible with the size screws you will be using to secure it to the wall.

5. Sand the entire hook with sandpaper, and clean it off with a towel. Make sure you leave no sawdust behind, as it will affect the paint line.

(Continued)

6. When you have four completed wooden pieces, use the painter's tape or washi tape to create the design. (The portion of the branch under the tape will remain its natural color.) Press the edges of the tape securely to the wood, removing any gaps or air bubbles, to ensure clean and crisp edges.

7. Dip the exposed portion of the branch into the paint and allow any excess to drip off. If you missed any spots, you can dip the branch again, or simply touch up with a brush.

8. Allow the hooks to dry for at least 24 hours, then peel off the painter's tape. Mount the hooks to the wall using screws and any other anchoring materials needed to keep the hooks secure.

WAYS TO USE THEM

* Instead of dipping the hook in paint, paint the entire hook for a more dramatic color statement.

* Use black or white paint for a clean, minimalist touch.

* Create a jewelry rack for necklaces and earrings by drilling the branch hooks into a wooden backing to hang on the wall.

* Dip the branches in diluted paint for a translucent effect.

* Use a high-gloss acrylic paint to create a more noticeable sheen.

13

a magazine for the
creative and curious

COLOR-BLOCKED
STONE PAPERWEIGHTS

DIFFICULTY
LEVEL

Let's face it: Most of us probably aren't working at a desk outside, in need of heavy paperweights to protect a pile of papers from gusty winds. But we just love bringing a touch of the outdoors in, and these color-blocked stones make the perfect decorative accent to any creative work area.

MATERIALS

* Several smooth-surfaced river rocks or garden stones
* Acrylic craft paint in your choice of colors

TOOLS

* Painter's tape or washi tape
* Sponge brush
* Parchment paper
* Towel

WHAT WE USED

* Found garden rocks
* Americana Acrylic Paint in Spa Blue, Zinc, and Terra Coral
* Ceramcoat Acrylic Paint in Yellow

Instructions

1. Wash the stones in warm, soapy water. Rinse and dry them thoroughly.

2. When the stones are dry, use painter's tape or washi tape to create the design. (The portion of stone under the tape will remain its natural color.) Layer pieces of tape at an angle to create points, or adhere a piece of tape in an unbroken line around the stone to create solid blocks of color.

3. Press the edges of the tape securely to the stone, removing any gaps or air bubbles, to ensure clean and crisp edges.

4. When you are satisfied with the tape pattern, sponge a few coats of acrylic craft paint onto the surface of the rock. Allow the paint to dry between coats.

5. When you are happy with the paint coverage and you are certain that the paint is dry, peel the tape from the stone to reveal the color blocks and shapes.

FRIENDLY PORCELAIN EGG CUPS

Egg cups are a pretty old-fashioned breakfast table accessory, but we are always interested in combining vintage pieces with modern ideas. In true Assemble fashion, we put a happy twist on a simple white egg cup. Using an easy transfer technique and a porcelain pen, you can make your breakfast smile—or frown or sport a beard and bow tie—whatever you like!

MATERIALS

* Porcelain egg cups
* Black fine-tip porcelain paint pen

TOOLS

* Pencil
* Tape
* Friendly Porcelain Egg Cups templates (pp. 88–89; see also Transferring Templates, p. 15)

WHAT WE USED

* Crate & Barrel® classic egg cups
* Pebeo Porcelaine 150 Paint Marker in Anthracite Black

Note: We hand-drew some extra accessories, such as the glasses and bandana.

Instructions

1. Photocopy the Friendly Porcelain Egg Cups templates.

2. Cut out each of the pieces, and play around with different combinations until you find a face you love.

3. When you decide on a design, rub the back side of the photocopy image with a graphite pencil. Make sure you cover the area behind the outline well—holding the sheet up to a light source can help.

4. Tape the printed pieces onto the surface of the egg cup, exactly where you want them, graphite side down.

5. Trace the lines with the pencil. This will transfer a faint line of graphite in the shape of the design onto the cup. Remove the paper templates.

6. Trace the graphite marks transferred to the egg cup with a black porcelain paint pen.

7. Let the ink dry for 24 hours and, if indicated on the pen's package directions, bake the jars in the oven at the appropriate temperature to set the ink.

TIP

Although these inks are labeled as permanent, we recommend hand washing your cups to prevent fading and wear.

JAPANESE STAB BOUND GUEST BOOK

Bookbinding classes were some of our students' favorites. They loved learning a practical new skill and creating a finished product that can be used as a journal, sketchbook, or wedding guest book. We like the idea of using this horizontal blank book as a visitor's book—with notes from all of the people who pass through your home. What a great way to remember coffee dates with old friends or the time your relatives flew in for the holidays.

MATERIALS

* **75 sheets 8½-in. by 5½-in. cardstock (80 lb. or similar)**
* **1 sheet 17⅞-in. by 5½-in. cover-weight paper**
* **Embroidery thread or hemp or linen thread, 3 yards**

TOOLS

* **Metal ruler**
* **Pencil**
* **Scissors**
* **Bone folder**
* **Screw punch, awl, or ⅛-in. hole punch**
* **Sewing needle**
* **Japanese Stab Bound Guest Book Jig template (p. 90)**
* **Tape**

WHAT WE USED

* **4-ply prewaxed linen thread in Black**
* **Fabriano® Tiziano 160gsm paper in Rose for cover**
* **Paper Source A9 80 lb. cardstock Pure White for interior pages (75 sheets)**

Instructions

1. Photocopy the jig template, and cut it out.

2. Stack the interior pages. Line up the edges of the jig and the pages. Use the screw punch to punch all nine holes into the sheets. If needed, split the sheets into sections you can punch through.

3. When you have completed punching holes, put the interior pages aside and begin making the cover.

4. Measure and mark two lines on the inside of the cover, 8½ in. from each edge. Then score each line using a bone folder. Fold and tightly crease both of those lines, which will create the outer spine for your book.

(Continued)

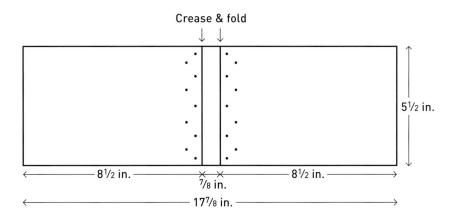

5. For the back cover, butt the jig template up to the crease on the right side of the sheet, and punch the holes. For the front cover, flip the jig over and butt the template against the crease on the left side, and punch the holes.

Note: The front will be folded over your interior pages, so you want to be sure the holes line up.

6. Place the interior pages snugly inside the cover, and prepare to sew the spine.

7. Thread the needle. Group the first 25 pages together and feed the needle under them until you reach the starting hole. Bring the needle up through the starting hole to come out the top of the stack. Doing this will hide the knot inside the pages instead of on the back cover. You should leave a 6-in.-long tail inside the interior pages to tie off at the end. Tape the tail in place on the page to keep it from slipping.

Note: The red lines in the illustration show the thread you will see on the front of the cover. The gray lines show what is on the back side.

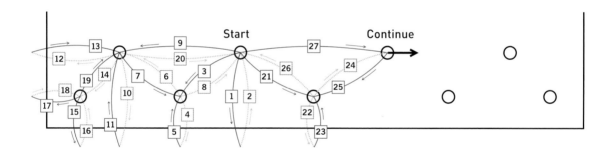

8. Continue to follow the step-by-step diagram, sewing around the entire spine in numerical order until the spine is completely threaded and you reach the place where you began. Find the starting tail, then thread the needle into the book to that same page you started at, tie a knot, and trim the tail.

TEMPLATES

SCANDINAVIAN MINI BLANKET CROSS STAMP

Use with project on p. 26.

Copy at 100%.

SKETCHED SALT & PEPPER JARS

Use with project on p. 34.

Copy at 100%.

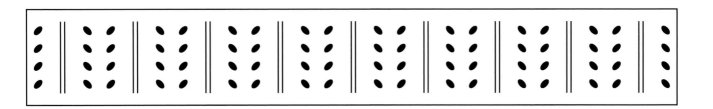

TEMPLATES

STENCILED COCKTAIL NAPKINS

Use with project on p. 39.

Copy at 200%.

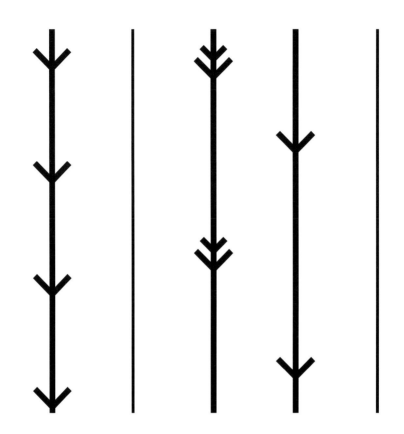

HONEYCOMB LINOLEUM BLOCK STAMPS

Use with projects on p. 47 and p. 50.

Copy at 100%.

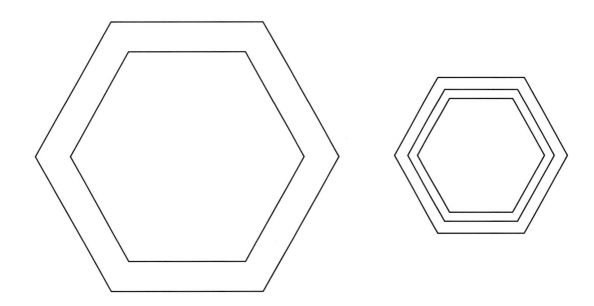

TEMPLATES

MATCHBOX CONFETTI BOXES

Use with project on p. 54.

Copy at 100%.

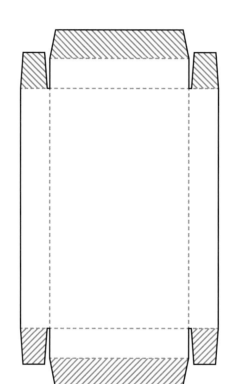

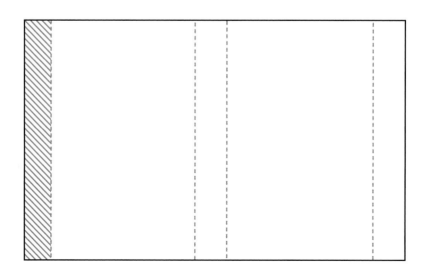

MINI ADVENTURE LOGS JIG

Use with project on p. 64.

Copy at 100%.

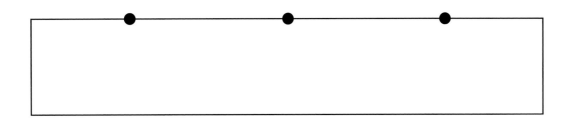

MINI ADVENTURE LOGS PATTERNS

Use with project on p. 64.

Copy at 133%.

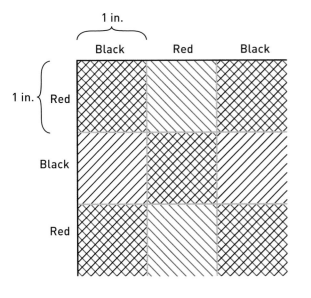

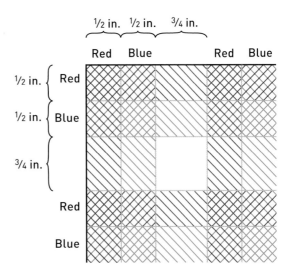

(Continued)

TEMPLATES

MINI ADVENTURE LOGS PATTERNS

Use with project on p. 64.

Copy at 133%

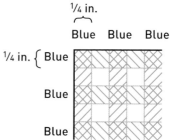

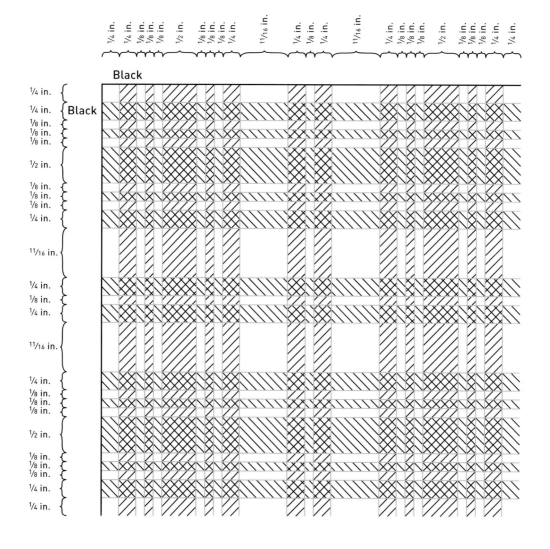

CAMPFIRE STORYTELLING STONES

Use with project on p. 68.

Copy at 100%.

TEMPLATES

FRIENDLY PORCELAIN EGG CUPS

Use with project on p. 76.

Copy at 100%.

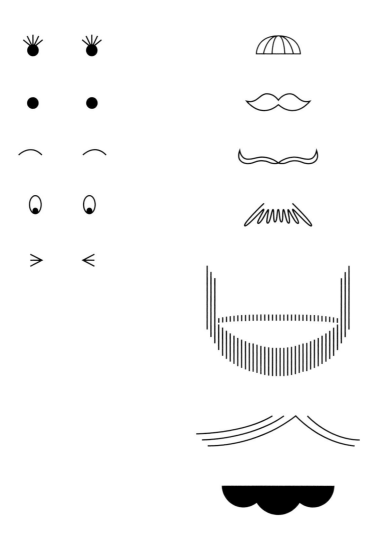

TEMPLATES

JAPANESE STAB BOUND GUEST BOOK JIG

Use with project on p. 78.

Copy at 100%.